Clinician's Guide

This book was written to provide clinicians with general knowledge and specific strategies for counseling patients on Buprenorphine medications. Much of what is contained in this guide is based on personal experiences and observations over the last 6 years. I have worked closely with Buprenorphine prescribers in developing and maintaining successful Suboxone programs, and have counseled many MAT patients.

I am in no way inferring that the other FDA approved medications for treating substance use disorders are not effective, just that I have not had much experience working with them yet.

Counseling patients in Medication Assisted Treatment (MAT) programs involves a shift in thinking that takes individualized treatment planning to a whole new level. This requires both the counselor and physician to remain open minded and aware of where the patient is in their individual recovery process. Regular communication between physician and counselor is beneficial, however the most important thing is that the counselor and physician have a similar understanding of how this treatment process works.

I often use the analogy of Selective Serotonin Reuptake Inhibitor (SSRI) medications that are prescribed for depression and anxiety. The first phase of treatment is successful when that patient is taking their SSRI medication, experiencing symptom relief, and regaining emotional stability. Counselors are then able, with therapy, to teach them how to identify and correct impaired thinking and behavior patterns. The patterns of negative self-talk and self-defeating behaviors that have kept the anxiety or depression alive and active.

This is also the time to work on improving strategies for coping with uncomfortable feelings as well as stress reduction.

The main concern at this phase of the process is not how quickly clinicians can taper them off the medication, in fact it is the opposite. Counselors teach them the importance of medication compliance and correct dosing. Basically, we teach them to make sure that they stay on their medications and take them as prescribed. This allows the counselor to work at a slower pace knowing that the patient is safe and stable.

This is the same approach that should be utilized when working with medications used to treat addiction. When an opiate addicted patient takes Buprenorphine as prescribed, they feel well. They are not impaired and the risk of death by accidental overdose has been nullified. Now the counselor can take their time and slowly help the patient build a meaningful and productive recovery life style.

In the case of SSRI medications, many patients get to a point where they can discontinue their medications completely. Some are able, to manage their depression or anxiety with the modifications that they made in their thinking and behaviors during counseling. However, some patients will need to take medications indefinitely.

Again, it is the same with patients taking Buprenorphine. With the help of counseling, many patients will learn how to manage their triggers and develop healthy recovery lifestyles and will taper off their medications. Others will need to be on Buprenorphine indefinitely.

That is why individualized treatment planning is so important. The doctor, counselor, and patient, need to understand the process. Unfortunately, that is often not the case. A better job needs to be done of reducing the stigmas surrounding Buprenorphine treatment. Doctors and counselors need to continue to collaborate and provide a more consistent and effective healthcare delivery system to the opiate addicted patient.

Clinician's Guide for Medication Assisted Treatment or MAT

Counseling Patients on Suboxone and Other Buprenorphine Medications

Developed by

Tom Diffenderfer LADAC II, QCS

Tom Diffenderfer LADAC II, QCS
Recovery Consulting Service
www.recoveryconsult.com
tom@recoveryconsult.com
615.904.9338
Copyright August 2017

Some Basic Principles

1. The therapeutic relationship takes on a different feel, but is more important than ever. The reason is due to the length of the counseling. The counselor may be working with this patient for years. Most addiction counselors are used to seeing a patient for several weeks or maybe up to 2 months. This is not the case with MAT patients. Counselors will see them less frequently, but for a much longer duration.

2. The counseling is slower paced. Once the client is stabilized on the medication they have no withdrawal symptoms and minimal cravings. They are feeling well. Most are functioning fine and are safe. The treatment retention rate is high. According to the National Institute of Health, 75% of patients receiving Buprenorphine treatment are still in recovery a year later.

3. There is no tolerance. Buprenorphine has a ceiling affect. Once the patient is comfortable on a specific dose of Buprenorphine, they will remain comfortable without requiring a dosage increase. They will not crave or need more, no matter how long they are on the medicine.

4. The medication has a long half-life and can last for 36 hours without major withdrawal symptoms.

5. The main goal is to help the patient place their Substance Use Disorder in remission. This is achieved by eliminating 10 of the 11 DSM-V criteria. The only remaining positive criteria will be withdrawal. If the patient abruptly discontinues Buprenorphine they will experience withdrawal. However, a patient with physical dependence alone, does not meet criteria for Substance Use Disorder.

6. Integrated service options and individualized counseling plans are two prevailing concepts in this guide. Everything that can be helpful is on the table. From medications that manage withdrawal and cravings, to psychiatric medications and cognitive therapies, this guide embraces the latest scientific advancements.

From essential oils and meditation, to 12 step meetings, yoga, nutrition and exercise, counselors can promote integration. For far too long these various practices have been separated by ingrained belief systems.

7. Every patient is unique and individual. It is the counselor's mission to work for the patient and help them develop their own unique recovery lifestyle.

Important topics that opiate addicted patients will need to address:

*Discontinue misusing problematic substances
*Learn about brain chemistry and how to help the brain heal
*Adopt new thinking and behaviors to avoid slips and relapse
*Develop strategies to manage triggers and cravings
*Improve coping skills to deal with unhealthy anxiety, stress, and anger
*Adopt a more peaceful lifestyle
*Develop enjoyable hobbies and interests
*Live with purpose and passion

Each counseling session features a discussion of changes, challenges and progress made since the last meeting. The remainder of the session consists of reviewing and working on the chapters in the workbook. The decision on how many counseling sessions are required should be based on the patient's current needs and then agreed upon by both counselor and patient. The number of sessions necessary is flexible and can be increased or decreased as situations change and progress is made. Anywhere between 4 to 12 sessions per month is a typical starting point. During the long-term maintenance period, 1 or 2 sessions per month is often appropriate.

Most experienced doctors will require verification that their patients are attending counseling on a regular basis. Some doctors may have in-house counseling services, many do not.

Group counseling is helpful for normalization, sharing of ideas, and social support. However, a large portion of the counseling will take place in one on one settings. Individual counseling can help the patient develop a life with passion, purpose and peace.

First Contact

Counseling begins with the first phone contact. Some of the patients that call the counselor will already be seeing a prescriber and are stable on Buprenorphine. If this is the case, then it can be as simple as scheduling them an intake appointment for counseling. Others will be reaching out for the first time, and in varying stages of withdrawal. They may be scared, anxious, agitated, physically sick or all the above. Don't underestimate the importance of this first phone contact. Not to be overly dramatic, but the next 10 to 15 minutes can be life-saving. Although extremely uncomfortable, opiate withdrawal is not life threatening. However, overdose can be fatal. A well-trained clinician should take the call.

The goal is to get the individual into treatment as quickly as possible without losing them. Begin discussing a plan of action. Friendly, warm and compassionate are important traits, along with confidence and motivation. The counselor's confidence that the plan will work, and their motivation to help, are contagious. Confidence and motivation can instill hope in the patient.

Ask the caller this question. If you stop taking opiates for a day or two do you start to get sick? If the answer is yes, then here are two options: Inpatient withdrawal management followed by counseling, or outpatient Buprenorphine with counseling. As the counselor explains these two options, they continue to affirm and motivate. Counselors can help reduce shame by freely discussing addiction as a disease while making comparisons to treatment for other chronic diseases such as diabetes or hypertension. Which option to select is a deeply personal decision that needs to be made by the patient.

Before we go any further it needs to be mentioned that prior to receiving treatment calls, the counselor needs to be well trained in how to solicit information and provide referrals. If not working in an inpatient facility or doctor's office, then It is imperative the counselor develop solid relationships with both. The counselor needs to be able to make referrals quickly and efficiently. Remember, if the patient is experiencing cravings, the clock is ticking before they use again. Using always increases the risk of overdose. Same day or next day referrals are best

5

The caller will often ask the counselor questions and solicit their advice or opinion. Counselors need to be able to provide them with current and updated information about their choices.

Inquire about health insurance and other financial resources. For some individuals that do not have health insurance, inpatient treatment will not be an option due to the high cost.

Listed are some other factors to consider as we help the patient decide how to move forward:

1. Their age, the duration and severity of their drug misuse, and the number of previous attempts at recovery, are important information. Patients who have had years of severe opiate misuse and have already tried inpatient treatment, may be good candidates for MAT.

2. Do they have legitimate chronic pain issues? Some opiate addicted patients have chronic pain issues that will last a lifetime. If they can manage their pain with non-narcotic pain medicine and Buprenorphine, MAT can be a very good option.

3. Are they on probation or parole? An individual with Opioid Use Disorder who is on probation or parole should consider remaining on Buprenorphine at least until they complete their legal requirements. Often patients in the criminal justice system become overwhelmed with cravings and relapse. Relapse leads to a positive drug screen, which leads to incarceration and or extended probation. The cycle keeps revolving. Once on Buprenorphine, the cravings are eliminated and the patient stands a much better chance of completing their legal requirements. The patient can move on with their recovery life.

4. Do they have pending legal charges that could result in jail time? Many jails and prisons don't allow Buprenorphine use. In this situation starting an individual who may be incarcerated soon on Buprenorphine, may not be appropriate.

5. Do they have a co-occurring mental health issue? Patients with a co-occurring diagnosis have a higher relapse rate due to the struggles associated with managing several brain diseases. There has been a lot of success when patients are taking both Buprenorphine and SSRI medications. This combination works well for many patients.

6. Are they in a position where they could go to an inpatient center for 1 to 4 weeks? Some individuals are in a situation where they will be able to get away for several weeks and work on their recovery. Others are not. Due to lack of child care or employment situations, Buprenorphine with outpatient counseling might be the best option for them.

7. Do they have a stable recovery environment? If the patient doesn't have a safe place to live due to physical or verbal abuse, then inpatient may be their best option. Or, if they live in an environment where there is steady drug use taking place, or they are homeless, then outpatient counseling is probably not appropriate. Some individuals will choose to go to inpatient treatment, but many will decide to enroll in Buprenorphine treatment and outpatient counseling.

The focus of this guide is to provide information on outpatient counseling with patients on Buprenorphine.

Counseling Patients on Buprenorphine

The key point is, if the patient continues to take the Buprenorphine according to their prescribed dose, they are safe from overdose. The patient will feel well without symptoms or cravings.

According to the Surgeon General's 2016 report on Addiction, there were over 33,000 deaths due to opiate overdose in 2016 alone. That number is more than auto accidents and gun violence. Any chance of overdose on a Buprenorphine and Naloxone combination (Suboxone, Bunavail, or Zubsolv) is almost nonexistent.

Suboxone, Bunavail, and Zubsolv, are the FDA approved Buprenorphine and Naloxone combinations. Suboxone was the first and remains the most widely prescribed. While the Buprenorphine is managing cravings and withdrawal, the Naloxone acts as a deterrent. This means that while a patient is being managed by one of these medications, if they choose to use other opiates, they will not get the euphoric feeling or high they are searching for. Their thinking goes something like this, If I'm not going to feel the high, then why bother to waste the money?

Withdrawal is the patient's enemy and greatest fear. Grown men breakdown in tears at the thought of having to go through withdrawal again. You see, opiate withdrawal is a horrible experience: Loss of control of their bodies and emotions, muscles cramp and twitch, uncontrollable diarrhea and vomiting, hot flashes, extreme anxiety and confusion, can't sleep but can't stay awake, flu-like symptoms x10, you get the picture. And this can go on for days. The body and mind is craving and screaming for opiates because opiates will stop the madness. However, so will Buprenorphine because it is a partial agonist opiate. Which means that it can stop the cravings and withdrawal symptoms without producing the intense euphoria or high.

"This medicine is a miracle", is a statement that counselors may hear many times from patients new to MAT.

Most MAT patients have experienced horrible withdrawal symptoms in the past, and many are beginning to feel withdrawal coming on as they arrive for their first visit to the doctor.

Within 30 minutes after taking the medicine they are beginning to feel relief, with the full effect in an hour. The topic of withdrawal will be an on-going discussion between the counselor and the MAT patient.

The delivery system for MAT lacks consistency. The programs vary from doctor to doctor and from counselor to counselor. The inconsistency of the delivery system inspired this guide.

From daily dosing strategies, to length of the maintenance phase of treatment, there are many different opinions. When to taper, how to taper, and if to taper at all, are questions best worked through as a team. The team, of course, is the patient, doctor, and counselor.

Hopefully consistency of treatment will improve over the next several years. After all, many if not most patients, doctors and counselors are new to MAT. We are going through a huge learning curve, an evolution in addiction treatment. However, with a knowledgeable and motivated team the results can be amazing.

Some doctors will require the patient to see them weekly, bi-weekly, or move quickly to a one visit per month maintenance phase. The counseling options can be anything from IOP, LIOP, bi-monthly or monthly.

Counseling is essential. Remember, there is no magic pill. Even though the medicine works wonders, most patients have had multiple years of impaired thinking and self-defeating behaviors. They are highly sensitized to triggers and cues. Their brain chemistry has been altered. They are entering a lengthy journey to emotional and physical wellness, and will need a guide.

It needs to be mentioned that the recovery journey has many paths. Some that I am aware of and others I am not. This guide sticks to what has been shown to be successful when working with patients on Buprenorphine combinations.

The MAT Counselor is multi-faceted. The seasoned counselor working with patients on Buprenorphine, knows how to flow between therapist, teacher, motivational coach, and role model or guide.

Once the patient is stable on Buprenorphine, the counseling begins. At the first session, we will take care of any intake paperwork and get a release signed for the patient's Buprenorphine prescriber. On the release, make sure to include a fax number or email address as counselors will be contacting the doctor's staff to verify counseling attendance. On the following page is a simple sample form that can be faxed to the prescriber's staff. The goal is to maintain a motivated efficient team. Stress team work often with the patient, the doctor, the physician's staff, and any involved family.

This is to verify that the individual listed below participated in a counseling session with

_____ for the treatment of Opioid Use Disorder.

Date of counseling: _____

Patient's name: _____

Follow up counseling recommendation:

1 session per week   _____

2 sessions per month   _____

1 session per month   _____

Account status: Paid in full

Staff signature and credentials:

Also during their first visit, provide them with the patient workbook and spend several minutes reviewing it with them. This is followed by casual open discussion. Get to know them. Learn about their interests and hobbies. Explore some short and long-term goals. Remember, the counselor and patient may be working together for years.

The 12 Steps

The 12 step programs of AA and NA are the largest, most effective support groups in the world for substance use disorders. These meetings are free and easy to find. In many communities, there are 12 step meetings offered 365 days a year. The recovering patient can even attend live meetings online at www.intherooms.com. The in the rooms website is a great resource for those wanting to explore 12 step recovery methods. The 12 step programs continue to provide unparalleled help, support, and a way of life for millions of recovering people. Although a long-time staple of addiction treatment, 12 step meetings are not for everybody, and some will choose a different path.

Counselors must be careful not to let their own beliefs about the 12 step programs influence their usefulness to the patient.

As counselors, we should be able to provide literature and education on the programs. Counselors can assist the patient with working the 12 steps if that is what the patient chooses to do. However, with today's advances in science, medications and therapy, patients are fortunate to have several different options to choose for their recovery.

Some patients will recover using only 12 step programs. Others will choose to take addiction medication and attend 12 step meetings. Many patients recover using Buprenorphine and counseling, having never attended 12 step meetings. Still other MAT patients find support in church, family, or other non-drug using friends. There are lots of good recovery apps. and websites as well.

Remember, as long as they take their medication as prescribed and attend counseling, they are safe from overdose, withdrawal and cravings. The average Buprenorphine patient will be in counseling at least one year and usually multiple years. There is plenty of time to help the patient develop a meaningful enjoyable recovery lifestyle.

Reduce the Fear of Withdrawal

This is where it gets tricky. Even a patient who is highly motivated for a successful recovery remains extremely fearful of going into withdrawal. They have developed a hyper-sensitivity to bodily fluctuations. If they start to sweat or have a muscle twitch or if they become tired, they immediately think that they are going into withdrawal and want to take a small piece of their medicine. The patient doesn't realize that everybody sweats, gets tired or may have a muscle twitch or cramp. Counselors need to remind them repeatedly, that it is only anxious thinking. It is not possible to go into withdrawal due to the Buprenorphine's long half-life.

Let's use an analogy of blood pressure medications. Once an individual's blood pressure is stabilized they don't self-medicate and take a small piece of hypertension medicine every time they feel anxious or flushed. Just allow the medication to work.

Remember, the medication has a ceiling effect and once stabilized on a particular dose, they will rarely need more and won't feel any different effect if they do take more. Many patients have developed this anxious thinking and it can take months of working with them until this thinking pattern is corrected.

Most patients will need regular affirmation and motivation. Patients need reassurance that the medicine works, and they will not experience withdrawal if they continue to take the medicine as prescribed. Counselors will quickly learn that one of the patient's prime motivations for recovery is fear of withdrawal. Generally speaking, this is a good thing. However, counselors will spend a lot of time helping the patients develop a more realistic view moving forward.

Next is a discussion about other potentially addicting substances. The patients may be feeling well or normal on Buprenorphine. However, they are used to getting high and experiencing that euphoric feeling. Many individuals are used to using substances to manage stress and self-medicate other uncomfortable feelings.

Even though the cravings are gone, and patients know they cannot take opiates, they may decide it would be ok to take something else. Marijuana, alcohol, or benzodiazepine are the usual suspects. Here the counselor may need to provide education about the dangers of switching from one addicting substance to another. Any benzodiazepine use should be discontinued under the supervision of a doctor. Benzodiazepines can be dangerous mixed with Suboxone and other Buprenorphine medications. Some doctors will have a low tolerance for drug screens that come back positive for benzodiazepine.

Most of the seasoned doctors will drug test every month. Since marijuana stays in the system for up to a month, this will also need to be discontinued. Some patients that do not have Alcohol Use Disorder, will have an occasional alcohol drink, but never to intoxication and only occasionally.

Most of the patients discontinue their alcohol consumption altogether. Taking Buprenorphine seems to help make it easier for the patient to stop using other substances, however this needs to be a part of the counseling plan. The brain is beginning to heal from the years of opiate use, and the goal is for the individual to become as emotionally well as possible.

Discontinuing the use of any other addicting substance is the best course of action here. The doctor should also test to make sure that Buprenorphine is in the patient's system. This will cut down on patient diversion of medication.

An underground market for Buprenorphine exists. Opiate addicted individuals are so afraid of going into withdrawal, that if they run out of their opiates, they will try to get Buprenorphine to hold them over until they can get their drug of choice. There are a small percentage of people who will try to abuse Buprenorphine, but most will take it to avoid withdrawal. A doctor and counselor working together can often identify patient diversion.

We need to assist the patients with reducing their fear of withdrawal while maintaining the correct dosing schedule. Once induction has been completed and the patients are stable, they will work out a dosing schedule with the doctor. For Suboxone, it will normally start at 16 milligrams per day, or two Suboxone films. Some patients will start with 8 milligrams. On a rare occasion, the doctor may start a patient on 24 milligrams per day. The doctors will normally recommend dosing once to twice daily. Patients that are in the process of a taper should move to one dose daily as soon as they can comfortably do so.

How Addiction Affects the Brain

Helping the MAT patients understand how their brain chemistry has been affected, is an important part of counseling. Here is a great explanation from the website www.helpmegetoffdrugs.com

The one property all addictive substances share is an ability to manipulate the brain's natural reward circuit in order to induce feelings of pleasure or relieve distress.

The reward circuit is designed to reinforce life-sustaining activities, such as eating and sex. Engaging in these activities stimulates neurons just above the brainstem to release dopamine into an area of the brain called the nucleus accumbens. The increased dopamine activity in the nucleus accumbens causes feelings of euphoria. Through this reward process, humans and other animals are taught to favor and therefore prioritize behaviors essential for their survival.

Increased dopamine activity also prompts the creation of a lasting memory associating the pleasurable feelings with the circumstances and settings under which they occur. In effect, these memories (also called conditioned associations) supplement the brain's positive reinforcement of certain behaviors.

From that point on, previously neutral stimuli will evoke or "trigger" memories of the reward experience. In the case of opioids, when the opioid molecule binds to the mu receptors in the brain, it initiates the same biochemical sequence and dopamine release normally reserved for life-saving behaviors. The rewarding effects of drugs of abuse come from large and rapid upsurges in dopamine, a neurochemical critical to stimulating feelings of pleasure and to motivating behavior.

The rapid dopamine "rush" from drugs of abuse mimics but greatly exceeds in intensity and duration the feelings that occur in response to such pleasurable stimuli as the sight or smell of food, for example.

Repeated exposure to such large, drug induced dopamine surges has the insidious consequence of ultimately blunting the response of the dopamine system to everyday stimuli. Thus, the drug disturbs a person's normal hierarchy of needs and desires and substitutes new priorities concerned with procuring and using the drug.

Drug abuse also disturbs the brain circuits involved in memory and control over behavior. Memories of the drug experience can trigger craving as can exposure to people, places, or things associated with former drug use. Stress is also a powerful trigger for craving. Control over behavior is compromised because the affected frontal brain regions are what a person needs to exert inhibitory control over desires and emotions.

That is why addiction is a brain disease. As a person's reward circuitry becomes increasingly dulled and desensitized by drugs, nothing else can compete with them food, family, and friends lose their relative value, while the ability to curb the need to seek and use drugs evaporates. Ironically and cruelly, eventually even the drug loses its ability to reward, but the compromised brain leads addicted people to pursue it anyway, anyway; the memory of the drug has become more powerful than the drug itself.

To summarize, here are a list of the important topics that counselors may have to review with their patients often during their recovery journey:

1. Help reduce the fear of withdrawal
2. Affirm and motivate / the medication and counseling plan work
3. Stop the self-medication
4. Educate on dopamine and natural highs
5. Review chapters in the workbook
6. Have a good time. Help the brain to heal with exercise and enjoyable activities
7. Continue to assess for co-occurring disorders and stuck points
9. Help the patient process the decision on when to do a medicine taper, or if a taper is appropriate.

Below is a list of topics that the patient and counselor can work on to resolve any problems before completing a medication taper.

Housing
Financial
Relationships
Employment
Legal matters
Hobbies and interests
Exercise and diet
Social

A Counseling Plan for Medication Assisted Treatment Or MAT

Patient/Counselor Workbook

Developed by
Tom Diffenderfer LADAC II, QCS

Patient/Counselor Workbook

The patient workbook was developed with the hope that both patient and healthcare provider could use it as a guide to promote recovery from Opioid Use Disorder. My goal was to create a hands-on workbook that touches on numerous recovery topics to be addressed in counseling. The workbook has two parts. In part one the reader will find twelve specific recovery strategies, along with various helpful concepts and tools for maintaining ongoing recovery. Part two of the workbook introduces the reader to the concepts of Struggle Reduction. Unhealthy anxiety is perhaps the most common trigger for slips and relapse among recovering MAT patients. The Art of Struggle Reduction presents a unique approach for decreasing and managing anxiety.

Since we may be working with the patient for months or years, we can always refer to various chapters in the workbook as situations arise. The counselor should become familiar with, and develop a working knowledge of the various strategies and concepts contained in part one of the workbook. Part two is a counseling theory designed to help reduce anxiety by developing a more peaceful lifestyle. This can be a bit more challenging to implement than the recovery strategies in part one. For the average MAT patient, waiting a period of 3 to 6 months prior to introducing struggle reduction concepts is recommended.

A Counseling Plan for Medication Assisted Treatment or MAT

Part One

Part Two

Forward

Opiate abuse and misuse has become a national epidemic in America with Tennessee being one of the hardest hit states. For over 23 years now, I have been providing assessment, counseling and education for this complex but treatable health condition. For the past five years, I have been collaborating with physicians in Middle Tennessee who are certified to prescribe Suboxone and other opioid replacement medications. This is Called Medication Assisted Treatment or MAT. The medication manages withdrawal and cravings allowing the patient to engage in substance abuse counseling, struggle reduction education, and relapse prevention education. The counseling and education focus on decreasing stress and anxiety while increasing emotional wellness, and recovery skills.

Medication Assisted Treatment continues to gain popularity as an effective option for treating Opioid Use Disorder. With that in mind, I decided to publish a patient/counselor workbook in 2014. At the time the book was written, there was little information available about appropriate counseling plans for MAT.

Since publishing the workbook in 2014, my patients & I have come across insights and observations, prompting a need to update the original edition. First and foremost:

1. Suboxone, Zubsolv and Bunavail, when appropriately used, are highly effective medications, and MAT is saving lives.
2. MAT works best when the treatment plan includes patient, physician and counselor collaborating in a team effort.
3. The delivery system needs improvement.
4. Some of the doctors, though well intentioned, are not experienced at working with opiate addicted clients and the unique set of challenges that they bring. Many MAT doctors are on a sharp learning curve.
5. Some well-meaning substance abuse counselors, frankly, have not kept up with all the changes and latest research in their own field. As a result, they have maintained one style fits all, outdated belief systems and strategies.
6. As a result, patients and society are not receiving enough consistent information about the disease of Opioid Use Disorder and how MAT maintenance and accompanying substance abuse counseling are supposed to work.

I think that now, more than ever, there exists a great opportunity for addiction counselors, physicians, mental health providers and patients to come together and learn from each other. My experience is that MAT physicians and mental health providers have been very open minded to work with me and the opiate dependent client. Everyone working together as a team provides positive results.

Medication Assisted Treatment for Opioid Use Disorder

From the Surgeon General's report "Facing Addiction in America" released in 2016

The combination of behavioral interventions and medications to treat substance use disorders is commonly referred to as Medication Assisted Treatment or MAT. MAT is a highly effective treatment option for individuals with alcohol and opioid use disorders. Studies have repeatedly demonstrated the efficacy of MAT at reducing illicit drug use and overdose deaths, improving retention in treatment, and reducing HIV transmission.

Some medications used to treat opioid use disorders can be used to manage withdrawal and as maintenance treatment to reduce craving, lessen withdrawal symptoms, and maintain recovery. These medications are used to help a patient function comfortably without illicit opioids or alcohol while balance is gradually restored to the brain circuits that have been altered by prolonged substance use.
Prescribed in this fashion, medications for substance use disorders are in some ways like insulin for patients with diabetes. Insulin reduces symptoms by normalizing glucose metabolism, but it is part of a broader disease control strategy that also employs diet change, education on healthy living, and self-monitoring. Whether treating diabetes or a substance use disorder, medications are best employed as part of a broader treatment plan involving behavioral health therapies and RSS, as well as regular monitoring.

The National Association of Alcohol and Drug Abuse Counselors (NAADAC) has recently released this information on the use of Buprenorphine in the treatment of Opioid Use Disorder:

*The goal of addiction treatment is always to assist a client in stopping his or her compulsive use of drugs or alcohol and progress to living a normal, functioning life. Medication assisted treatment for opioid use disorder can help clients achieve this goal.

*Addiction to opioids creates a myriad of negative effects to the addicted client, his or her family, friends, and society as a whole. Most of these devastating effects of opioid dependence are due to the illicit nature of the drug, debilitating side effects of constant use, and the dependent's inability to perform normal functions of society such as working and parenting. Removing negative effects of opioid use allows a client to live a normal life and contribute to society. Medication assisted treatment with opiate replacement medications can be highly effective for opiate dependent clients.

*If appropriately administered, medication assisted treatments for opioid dependence will not produce euphoric effects, but will help the person feel normal.

*An addiction to opioids and a physical dependence to a medication used to prevent withdrawal symptoms are not the same thing. Addiction and physical dependence are different. Addiction is defined by the pathological behaviors and compulsivity of use, not by the body's adaption to a medicine. Physical dependence is only one of 11 criteria that are required for a diagnosis of opiate use disorder (addiction). The following paragraph is an excerpt from the Clinical Guidelines for the Use of Buprenorphine in the Treatment of Opioid Addiction.

The following statement is from the Clinical Guidelines for Buprenorphine treatment as published by the U.S. DEPARTMENT OF HEALTH AND HUMAN SERVICES, Substance Abuse and Mental Health Services Administration Center for Substance Abuse Treatment:

*The design of long-term treatment depends in part on the patient's personal treatment goals and in part on objective signs of treatment success. Maintenance can be relatively short term (e.g., <12 months) or a lifetime process. Treatment success depends on the achievement of specific goals that are agreed on by both the patient and the physician.

Principles of Effective Treatment for Adults from the Surgeon General's report, Facing Addiction in America 2016

1. Addiction is a complex but treatable disease that affects brain function and behavior.

2. No single treatment is appropriate for everyone.

3. Treatment needs to be readily available.

4. Effective treatment attends to multiple needs of the individual, not just his or her drug abuse.

5. Remaining in treatment for an adequate period of time is critical.

6. Behavioral therapies—including individual, family, or group counseling-- are the most commonly used forms of drug abuse treatment.

7. Medications are an important element of treatment for many patients, especially when combined with counseling and other behavioral therapies.

8. An individual's treatment and services plan must be assessed continually and modified as necessary to ensure that it meets his or her changing needs.

9. Many drug-addicted individuals also have other mental disorders.

10. Medically assisted detoxification is only the first stage of addiction treatment and by itself does little to change long-term drug abuse.

11. Treatment does not need to be voluntary to be effective.

12. Drug use during treatment must be monitored continuously, as lapses during treatment do occur.

13. Treatment programs should test patients for the presence of HIV/AIDS, Hepatitis B and C, tuberculosis, and other infectious diseases, provide risk-reduction counseling, and link patients to treatment if necessary.

Substance Use Disorders and the Criminal Justice System

The criminal justice system in America has the difficult job of keeping us safe and maintaining order in our lawful society. With all the variables that are being thrown their way, the challenges are great. In general, I applaud their efforts. However just like the rest of society, they need to do a better job of understanding that substance use disorder is a disease of the brain.

When a person is convicted of an alcohol or drug related criminal offense, they often have a diagnosable substance use disorder. They are probably in need of addiction education, counseling, and in many cases medication. Instead they are often incarcerated and begin severe withdrawal and craving. Most times as soon as they are released, all they can think about is satisfying the overwhelming craving and obsession. They often begin using drugs again while on probation because they lack the skills to resist the cravings on their own.

Our proposed residential alternative sentencing facilities with access to MAT, are designed to help break the vicious cycle of incarceration, probation, positive drug test, followed by probation violation and incarceration. MAT can help manage the client's withdrawal symptoms, while they are completing any required jail time in a safe therapeutic environment. The client is also participating in therapy and developing an ongoing recovery plan for when they are discharged from the facility. This could have a major impact on recidivism, which in turn would help with jail overcrowding.

Integrated Service Options and Individualized Counseling Plans

Integrated service options and individualized counseling plans are two prevailing concepts in this guide. Everything that can be helpful is on the table. From medications that manage withdrawal and cravings to psychiatric medications and cognitive therapies, this guide embraces the latest scientific advancements. From essential oils and meditation, to 12 step meetings, yoga, nutrition and exercise counselors can promote integration. For far too long these various practices have been separated by ingrained belief systems. Every patient is unique and an individual. It is the counselor's mission to work for the patient to help them develop their own unique recovery lifestyle. Group counseling is helpful for normalization, sharing of ideas, and social support, however a large portion of counseling takes place in one on one settings, helping the patient develop a life with passion, purpose and peace.

The counseling plans proposed in this book are my opinions and observations developed from the 23 years I have spent working with opiate addicted patients. These counseling strategies, along with the medications, have been shown to be an effective treatment option for the disease of Opiate Use Disorder. Although I have seen success with these strategies, I am in no way suggesting that they are the only approach. The recovery journey has many paths.

MAT is a lengthy process that yields higher than average patient retention in recovery. This allows for the pace of counseling to be slower, often encompassing a wide range of short and long-term goals. The length of the maintenance phase of MAT needs to be highly individualized. Depending on circumstances and situations, some patients will complete a medication taper in less than a year, other patients may require long-term maintenance indefinitely, and for others this will be a life-long process.

Regardless of how long a patient receives medication our belief is that recovery from Substance Use Disorders should include the following:

*Discontinue misusing the problematic substance
*Adopt new thinking and behaviors to avoid slips and relapse
*Develop strategies to manage triggers and cravings
*Improve coping skills to deal with unhealthy anxiety, stress, and anger
*Adopt a more peaceful lifestyle
*Develop enjoyable hobbies and interests
*Live with purpose and passion

Each counseling session features a discussion of changes, challenges and progress made since the last meeting. The remainder of the session consists of reviewing and working on the chapters in the workbook. The decision on how many counseling sessions are required should be based on the patient's current needs and then agreed upon by both counselor and patient. The number of sessions necessary is flexible and can be increased or decreased as situations change and progress is made. Anywhere between 4 to 12 sessions per month is a typical starting point. During the long-term maintenance period, 1 or 2 sessions per month is often appropriate.

Healthy Recovery Boundaries

When we speak of boundaries as it relates to recovery from Opiate Use Disorder, we are referring to keeping your recovery safe and protected. Opiate dependents have become highly sensitized to certain people, places and things that remind them of drug use, and trigger drug using thoughts. One of the ways to manage this is to set boundaries with people, places and things that are a threat to your recovery. Utilizing appropriate healthy recovery boundaries is empowering, and helps you to gain control of your life again.

Establishing boundaries does not mean being judgmental of what other people choose to do. It is about firmly saying no to people, places and things that could threaten your sobriety.

Here are some examples of recovery boundaries that may need to be set:
Drug abusing friends, dealers, drug abusing partners or spouses.
Emotionally or physically abusive friends or family.
Nightclubs, bars, drug houses and anywhere there is a high risk of drug abuse taking place.

Begin saying yes to a positive, healthy, recovery environment, and say no to negative influences and triggers.

Spend some time thinking about what boundaries need to be set to protect your recovery, and write them down. Ask your counselor for help. You can practice establishing boundaries by using role play exercises.

_____

_____

_____

_____

_____

_____

_____

_____

_____

The Diseases of Substance Use and Co-occurring Disorders

Opioid use disorder is a chronic and progressive disease of the brain. At any given time, the disease is either active or in remission. The opiate dependents goal is to place their disease in remission and live a productive, meaningful life.

It is not so much about weak or strong, or good or bad. It is really about sick or well. Recovery from opiate addiction is a journey to wellness.

Co-occurring disorders refers to having two or more diseases of the brain, with at least one of the diseases being Substance Use Disorder. A couple of examples of co-occurring disorders are: Alcohol Use Disorder and Major Depression, or Opiate Use Disorder and Obsessive-Compulsive Disorder.

Many opiate dependents struggle with another mental illness as well. Some of the most common mental illnesses we see in addiction counseling are: Panic Disorder, Bi-polar Disorder, PTSD, OCD, Major Depression, Generalized Anxiety Disorder, and Social Phobia.

If you are experiencing any emotional distress, high anxiety, or depression be sure to talk to your counselor about it. They can help you understand what is going on and develop a plan of recovery. The counselor may also make referrals to other appropriate mental health care providers. Co-occurring disorders should be treated simultaneous.

Opioid use disorders and co-occurring disorders are all treatable. The most common forms of treatment are therapy, medication, or a combination of both.

Document any questions or concerns you may have and bring them to your next session.

_____

_____

_____

_____

_____

_____

_____

Recovery Literature and Online Support Sites

For many years, recovery literature has been a main stay in the treatment of addiction. Starting with the big book of AA, there have been many great books written on the topic of recovery from addiction. Add to that a growing number of recovery websites and apps that are now present on the internet These books, apps, and websites can be used as recovery maps or guides. However, like most topics available on the web, there is inaccurate and wrong information out there as well. Be especially wary of the Buprenorphine and Suboxone blog sites.

To successfully recover from addiction, the opiate dependent will need to make changes in certain beliefs and behaviors. Recovery literature and online support sites are some of the tools that educate and inform the recovering opiate abuser as to what needs to change and how to make those changes.

Here are some examples of popular recovery books that can be found in most inpatient and outpatient treatment settings: The Big Book of Alcoholics Anonymous, The Narcotics Anonymous Basic Text, Twelve Steps and Twelve Traditions, Co-dependent No More, The Language of Letting Go, A Day at a Time, The Addiction Recovery Skills Workbook and many others.

Your counselor should be well-versed on the various types of recovery and self-help books, apps and websites that are available, and can help you choose a good fit for your circumstances and beliefs.

A certain amount of humility and awareness may be required for you to reach the realization that change needs to happen, it is ok to ask for and receive help.

www.meditationalbums.com is a website that contains a large collection of recovery tools and support links that can be used in conjunction with this workbook.

The meditation albums site includes links to:
1. Recovery workbooks
2. Hypnotherapy sleep aides
3. Guided relaxation for anxiety
4. The Walk to Wellness exercise plan
5. Daily reflections
6. The largest global recovery support site
7. Live online recovery support meetings
8. Recovery speakers
9. Beginners Yoga
10. A smoking cessation group

Local and Online Support Groups

Family, friends, 12 step support groups, Spiritual and meditation groups, exercise classes, private therapy, and church are some of the supports that can be a valuable resource for ongoing recovery. Knowing that you are not alone, and that there are other people going through similar struggles can be very healing. If you have to let go of old drug using friends, there can initially be a void or a feeling of loneliness. Various types of support groups have been shown to provide a safe place to bond with others, as well as an avenue to learn what has worked for your peers. The old saying there is strength in numbers certainly applies to recovery from addiction. The 12 step programs of AA and NA are the largest, most effective support groups in the world for substance use disorders. These groups are free and easy to find. In many communities, there are 12 step meetings, 365 days a year. You can even attend live meetings online at www.intherooms.com. The in the rooms website is a great resource for those wanting to explore 12 step recovery methods. Your counselor can provide literature and education on the programs, as well as assist you with working the 12 steps if that is what you choose to do.

Although a long-time staple of addiction treatment, 12 step meetings are not for everybody, and some will choose a different path. Again, your counselor is well versed in the various types of support groups and will help you find something that will meet your needs.

Explain any experiences you may have had with support groups in the past, and what ideas you have moving forward.

_____

_____

_____

_____

_____

_____

_____

_____

_____

_____

Internal and External Triggers

A trigger is a stimulus which has been repeatedly associated with the preparation for, anticipation of, or use of drugs and/or alcohol. These stimuli include people, things, places, times of day, and emotional states. People, places, objects, feelings and times can cause cravings. An important part of recovery from addiction, involves stopping the craving process. Begin to identify your specific triggers, and learn to deal with them in a different way.

It takes effort to identify and stop a drug-use related thought. The further the thoughts are allowed to go; the more likely the individual is to use drugs.

Triggers, thoughts, and craving can run together. The usual "trigger" sequence, however, is as follows:
Trigger > Thought > Craving > Use

The key to dealing with this process, is to not allow it to start. Stopping the thought when it first begins, helps prevent it from building into a craving. Here are a few thought-stopping techniques: visualization, snapping, relaxation, calling someone, distraction (thought substitution), prayer, going to a 12-step meeting, reading recovery or spiritual literature, playing the "whole tape exercise."

In the space below list some of your primary internal and external triggers:

Internal (feelings) _____

_____

_____

_____

External (people, places and things) _____

_____

_____

_____

_____

Cognitive Rewiring

The brain becomes conditioned by repetition. Repeated thoughts or self-talk create pathways that can alter brain functioning. Thoughts and self-talk' affect mood. Therefore, scary thoughts, combined with self-talk that questions one's ability to cope, can create feelings of high anxiety and tension. While calming thoughts and affirming reassuring self-talk creates feelings of confidence and relaxation. The patterns of thinking and messages that you told yourself while in active addiction, were often impaired, unrealistic, negative and damaging. In recovery, we learn how to identify specific areas of impaired thinking and negative self-talk, challenge them, and then replace those thoughts and messages with something more realistic, supportive, and positive. This in turn has a major impact on mood and emotional well-being. Some of these patterns of impaired thinking have been with you a long time, and it will take repetition and persistence to change. It is well worth it. Another way to look at it is that you are rewiring your brain.

Using opioid replacement medications (like buprenorphine) can be especially helpful during this process. Since the medication helps manage withdrawal and cravings, and the maintenance phase of treatment is often lengthy, the individual has plenty of time to work on cognitive reframing.

Begin to pay attention to your specific negative thoughts and patterns of self-talk, and write them down. Then write down a realistic and affirming message to replace the old one.

Negative irrational thoughts and messages   Positive, realistic thoughts and messages

_____   _____

_____   _____

_____   _____

_____   _____

_____   _____

Negative irrational thoughts and messages   Positive, realistic thoughts and messages

_____   _____

_____   _____

_____

_____

_____

_____

_____

Negative irrational thoughts and messages

_____

_____

_____

_____

_____

Negative irrational thoughts and messages

_____

_____

_____

_____

_____

_____

_____

_____

_____

_____

Positive, realistic thoughts and messages

_____

_____

_____

_____

_____

Positive, realistic thoughts and messages

_____

_____

_____

_____

_____

Re-establishing Relationships

Addiction is a family disease. Not only is the individual with the illness affected, but the rest of the family can be affected as well. Co-dependency, dishonesty, resentments, feelings of guilt and shame, and unhealthy enabling are just a few of the issues that can occur in a family trying to recover from substance use disorder. Learning to trust the recovering substance abuser, may be the single biggest hurdle to overcome. It will take time to rebuild that trust. Remember, the best way for those in recovery to demonstrate that they can be trusted again, is to show with responsible action, not words.

Now that the opiate dependent is taking medicine to manage withdrawal and cravings, they feel normal again. It's hard for them to understand why everyone can't just let the past be the past and move forward. On the other hand, the family or significant other wants the opiate dependent to be "all better" right away. Patience for all involved is the recommended course of action.

Often time the family or significant others want to know how they can help or "fix" their addicted loved one. The loved ones can offer support, but ultimately, it falls on the shoulders of the opiate dependent to make and maintain the necessary changes to recover.

Licensed addictions counselors can help the individual and family work through many of these issues. The counselor will usually spend the first couple sessions working directly with the patient. After that, different family members or significant others are welcome to join some of the sessions. The counselor can provide helpful education and answer questions that the loved ones may have. Couples counseling is also available to foster better communication and compromise.

Do you feel that you and your family or significant other would benefit from family or couples counseling? Have you asked them and have they agreed to participate?

Write down any thoughts you may have on the subject. Include several things that you are willing to change about yourself to promote healing in your relationships.

_____

_____

_____

_____

_____

_____

Enjoyable Sober Activities

It is usually not enough to just stop abusing the drugs or alcohol. An addicted person can sometimes go days, weeks, even months without abusing drugs. They accomplish this with will power alone. However, when they begin using again, most will pick up where they left off. The addicted person quickly losing control of how much and how often they use.

A key element of maintaining long term sobriety is learning how to have fun and enjoy life again without abusing alcohol or drugs. When the drug misuse is stopped, the brain continues to heal. It begins producing more of the pleasure chemicals that are necessary to achieve natural highs. The goal is to not just achieve sobriety. It is more about developing a quality recovery lifestyle.

Think back to when you were a young child. Do you remember playing games with your friends, getting lost in an imaginary world? Or the excitement on the night before Christmas thinking about the joy that awaits you in the morning. The thrill of that first kiss or when your team wins the championship are all natural highs. Our brain chemistry provides us with a vast array of pleasurable experiences and feelings. We come completely equipped with everything we need to enjoy life. As our drug misuse continues to progress, we begin to develop the belief that we need an external substance or drug to experience joy. We can become so lost in our addiction that we feel we cannot survive without our substance. But that is the big lie. In truth, our brains will heal and we will return to enjoying life naturally again.

As addiction progresses, the process of getting and using the drugs becomes more and more of an obsession. This often robs us of our other interests and passions. There are many things to consider as you learn to develop quality sobriety. One of them is balance. Trying to achieve a healthy balance between work and play, as well as alone time and family, can be challenging. This is also the time to renew old hobbies and interests or acquire new ones. Rekindling the passion and meaning in life can be a wonderful journey. Fishing, camping, playing a musical instrument, travel, sewing, biking, sports, church, support groups, volunteering to help others, date night with your partner, gardening, photography, and taking a class are just a few of the endless number of things that people recovering from addiction enjoy.

Be careful not to fall into the rut of just working and sleeping. Ask your counselor for help and be willing to experience new things. Many opiate dependents develop all or nothing thinking. Allow your counselor to help you build an enjoyable quality sober lifestyle.

List some hobbies and interests that you would like to re-establish and some new interests you would like to pursue:

_____

_____

_____

Relaxation for Anxiety

High levels of unhealthy anxiety that lead to feelings of being overwhelmed is one of the number one causes of relapse for those recovering from opiate use disorder. As the anxious feelings become more uncomfortable, the urge to self-medicate by abusing drugs or alcohol often becomes too hard to resist. Regular practice of deep relaxation has been shown to help manage this type of anxiety.

We understand the many struggles that people in recovery have with anxiety. Counselors and therapists have been recommending various forms of guided visualization, progressive muscle relaxation and meditation for many years. They have long known that practicing this type of deep relaxation has emotional, physical and spiritual benefits.

Eight Good Reasons to Practice Deep Relaxation:

* Reduce anxiety and manage stress * Reduce frequency and intensity of panic attacks * Live a calmer life style with improved mood * Help prevent relapse for those in recovery * It feels good to be calm and at peace * Lower blood pressure and risk of stroke * add years to your life * Help getting to sleep

Visit **www.meditationalbums.com** to learn more about deep relaxation and meditation and to access audio presentations, downloads, and apps. that will help you achieve these deeper states of calm. Let your counselor know if you would like to try some hypnotherapy or guided relaxation at one of your sessions.

Relapse Prevention

After the opiate dependent stops abusing his or her drugs of choice, the goal then becomes relapse prevention. Many men and women with long-term sobriety use words like maintenance and remission. Opiate Use Disorder is a disease of the brain. The psychiatric Diagnostic and Statistical Manual 5th edition (DSMV), states that 3 months or more of continual recovery, constitutes partial remission. 12 months or more of sobriety indicates complete full remission. Long term sobriety or recovery, consists of placing the disease of addiction in remission and keeping it there.

This is where relapse prevention comes into play. The opiate dependent has lost the ability to control or stop their drug use, so it becomes critical to avoid relapse back into drug use and all of the negative consequences that come with it.

Below is a sample relapse prevention plan:

1. Understand relapse as a process, not an event.
The Relapse process starts long before the drug or drink are actually taken. Extended periods of agitation, restlessness, confusion, and a feeling of being "off track" are all indicators that your recovery could be in danger. Not talking about your feelings, increasing anxiety and a feeling of being overwhelmed can all be warning signs. If these warning signs are not dealt with, old thinking and behavior patterns often resurface. Manipulation, dishonesty, wanting to be in control can be examples of a recovery program that needs tending. The AA program calls it "stinking thinking." Eventually one will either get their recovery back on track or get so frustrated and deluded that they begin using drugs/alcohol again.

2. Increase participation in healthy activities.

What healthy activities can you increase? _____

_____

_____

_____

_____

3. Understand and address social pressures to use substances.

What boundaries need to be set and by who? _____

_____

_____

_____

4. Develop a supportive relapse prevention network (e.g., with significant others).

Make a list of those people in you relapse prevention network. _____

_____

_____

_____

5. Recognize relapse warning signs, including internal and external triggers.

Write a list of your internal and external triggers. _____

_____

_____

_____

6. Combat memories of drug abuse-associated euphoria.

Develop and learn how to play the whole tape (and then what) _____

_____

_____

_____

_____

7. Reinforce recollections of negative aspects of drug use.

Make a list of the negative aspects of drug/alcohol use. _____

_____

_____

_____

8. Avoid people, places, and things that might trigger drug use.

Create a list of people, places and things that might trigger drug/alcohol use. _____

_____

_____

_____

_____

9. Develop a list of pleasurable and rewarding alternatives to drug use.

_____

_____

_____

Overall Wellness

Much of what we have been talking about concerns emotional wellness. Those that have developed and maintained a healthy recovery have learned how to place their emotional well-being as their top priority. This does not mean that they are selfish or self-centered; quite the contrary, they know that they can't help anyone else if they don't keep themselves healthy. The old saying, "you can't give away what you don't have," certainly applies here.

We are all different. What one person needs to attend to in order to feel well can be different for someone else. Exercise, sleep, and diet all play a factor. Balance and boundaries are important components, as are hobbies and interests. Living a sober life of passion and purpose with realistic and affirming self-talk and achievable goals all help to reduce the risk of relapse.

Remember, if a drug addicted person stops abusing drugs and doesn't change anything else, they can become restless and discontented. Then, the thinking usually goes something like this. If this is what being sober is like, I'd rather just go get high. This is why developing a quality recovery lifestyle is so important. If that same person is enjoying their life and feeling good about themselves, their chances of relapse are greatly reduced. Your Counselor should know how to help recovering addicts develop productive, meaningful recovery lives. Talk to them. Ask questions. Ask for help.

List areas of concerns you have identified that you may need help with.

_____

_____

_____

_____

_____

_____

Follow Up Counseling

During this time of medication management, you have gotten to know your counselor, and he or she have gotten to know you. Within this relationship, healing has taken place. You have invested a lot of time and money into this, and what you have received for your efforts is a quality sober life. Your disease of addiction is in remission. But remember; recovery is not a destination, not a place that you get to. It is a way of life that you learn how to live. Like anyone else with a chronic disease, you must continue to walk the walk of recovery. Some of you may have already completed your medication taper, while others have realized that it may be months or longer that they will need to continue their medication.

The relationship you have built with your counselor is a valuable commodity. You are always welcome to schedule a session. If you reach a point in your life where there is struggle, don't hesitate to reach out to your counselor for help and guidance. The sessions can be just to touch base or for deeper struggles (empty nest, loss of employment, or other major life events).

If you relapse back into drug or alcohol use, don't let shame or pride keep you out there in active addiction. Your counselor understands that relapse is often another stage or learning period that can lead to sustained recovery in the end.

The Daily Self-report and Personal Inventory

The Daily self-report and personal inventory that begins on the next page, is an effective recovery tool for maintaining awareness of the here and now. Each day when you wake up, write down your feelings and thoughts. Follow this by documenting the things you would like to do from now until you go to sleep. Maintaining awareness of what is unfolding during each twenty-four hours helps us avoid excessive guilt about the past and worry about the future. Complete the day with a brief recap including challenges and achievements.

Repeating the self-report and personal inventory on a daily basis, helps add structure to our lives. We can learn to observe healthy or destructive patterns beginning to develop. Then, correct mistakes and change behaviors if needed. Above all else, maintaining focus on the present helps us avoid feeling overwhelmed by the accumulation of stress and anxiety.

We have included 30 daily self-reports and personal inventories. This will be sufficient for the first month. Feel free to make copies for ongoing use.

The Daily Self-report and Personal Inventory

Today I feel: _____

_____

_____

_____

Today I think: _____

_____

_____

_____

From now until I go to sleep tonight I will: _____

_____

_____

_____

Daily inventory

The last 24 hours I: _____

_____

_____

_____

_____

_____

_____

The Daily Self-report and Personal Inventory

Today I feel: _____

_____

_____

_____

Today I think: _____

_____

_____

_____

From now until I go to sleep tonight I will: _____

_____

_____

_____

Daily inventory

The last 24 hours I: _____

_____

_____

_____

_____

_____

_____

The Daily Self-report and Personal Inventory

Today I feel: _____

_____

_____

_____

Today I think: _____

_____

_____

_____

From now until I go to sleep tonight I will: _____

_____

_____

_____

Daily inventory

The last 24 hours I: _____

_____

_____

_____

_____

_____

The Daily Self-report and Personal Inventory

Today I feel: _____

_____

_____

_____

Today I think: _____

_____

_____

_____

From now until I go to sleep tonight I will: _____

_____

_____

_____

Daily inventory

The last 24 hours I: _____

_____

_____

_____

_____

_____

_____

The Daily Self-report and Personal Inventory

Today I feel: _____

_____

_____

_____

Today I think: _____

_____

_____

_____

From now until I go to sleep tonight I will: _____

_____

_____

_____

Daily inventory

The last 24 hours I: _____

_____

_____

_____

_____

_____

The Daily Self-report and Personal Inventory

Today I feel: _____

_____

_____

_____

Today I think: _____

_____

_____

_____

From now until I go to sleep tonight I will: _____

_____

_____

_____

Daily inventory

The last 24 hours I: _____

_____

_____

_____

_____

_____

The Daily Self-report and Personal Inventory

Today I feel: _____

_____

_____

_____

Today I think: _____

_____

_____

_____

From now until I go to sleep tonight I will: _____

_____

_____

_____

Daily inventory

The last 24 hours I: _____

_____

_____

_____

_____

_____

The Daily Self-report and Personal Inventory

Today I feel: _____

_____

_____

_____

Today I think: _____

_____

_____

_____

From now until I go to sleep tonight I will: _____

_____

_____

_____

Daily inventory

The last 24 hours I: _____

_____

_____

_____

_____

_____

_____

The Daily Self-report and Personal Inventory

Today I feel: _____

_____

_____

_____

Today I think: _____

_____

_____

_____

From now until I go to sleep tonight I will: _____

_____

_____

_____

Daily inventory

The last 24 hours I: _____

_____

_____

_____

_____

_____

_____

The Daily Self-report and Personal Inventory

Today I feel: _____

_____

_____

_____

Today I think: _____

_____

_____

_____

From now until I go to sleep tonight I will: _____

_____

_____

_____

Daily inventory

The last 24 hours I: _____

_____

_____

_____

_____

_____

The Daily Self-report and Personal Inventory

Today I feel: _____

_____

_____

_____

Today I think: _____

_____

_____

_____

From now until I go to sleep tonight I will: _____

_____

_____

_____

Daily inventory

The last 24 hours I: _____

_____

_____

_____

_____

_____

The Daily Self-report and Personal Inventory

Today I feel: _____

_____

_____

_____

Today I think: _____

_____

_____

_____

From now until I go to sleep tonight I will: _____

_____

_____

_____

Daily inventory

The last 24 hours I: _____

_____

_____

_____

_____

_____

_____

The Daily Self-report and Personal Inventory

Today I feel: _____

_____

_____

_____

Today I think: _____

_____

_____

_____

From now until I go to sleep tonight I will: _____

_____

_____

_____

Daily inventory

The last 24 hours I: _____

_____

_____

_____

_____

_____

_____

The Daily Self-report and Personal Inventory

Today I feel: _____

_____

_____

_____

Today I think: _____

_____

_____

_____

From now until I go to sleep tonight I will: _____

_____

_____

_____

Daily inventory

The last 24 hours I: _____

_____

_____

_____

_____

_____

The Daily Self-report and Personal Inventory

Today I feel: _____

_____

_____

_____

Today I think: _____

_____

_____

_____

From now until I go to sleep tonight I will: _____

_____

_____

_____

Daily inventory

The last 24 hours I: _____

_____

_____

_____

_____

_____

_____

The Daily Self-report and Personal Inventory

Today I feel: _____

_____

_____

_____

Today I think: _____

_____

_____

_____

From now until I go to sleep tonight I will: _____

_____

_____

_____

Daily inventory

The last 24 hours I: _____

_____

_____

_____

_____

_____

_____

The Daily Self-report and Personal Inventory

Today I feel: _____

_____

_____

_____

Today I think: _____

_____

_____

_____

From now until I go to sleep tonight I will: _____

_____

_____

_____

Daily inventory

The last 24 hours I: _____

_____

_____

_____

_____

_____

The Daily Self-report and Personal Inventory

Today I feel: _____

_____

_____

_____

Today I think: _____

_____

_____

_____

From now until I go to sleep tonight I will: _____

_____

_____

_____

Daily inventory

The last 24 hours I: _____

_____

_____

_____

_____

_____

_____

The Daily Self-report and Personal Inventory

Today I feel: _____

_____

_____

_____

Today I think: _____

_____

_____

_____

From now until I go to sleep tonight I will: _____

_____

_____

_____

Daily inventory

The last 24 hours I: _____

_____

_____

_____

_____

_____

The Daily Self-report and Personal Inventory

Today I feel: _____

_____

_____

_____

Today I think: _____

_____

_____

_____

From now until I go to sleep tonight I will: _____

_____

_____

_____

Daily inventory

The last 24 hours I: _____

_____

_____

_____

_____

_____

The Daily Self-report and Personal Inventory

Today I feel: _____

_____

_____

_____

Today I think: _____

_____

_____

_____

From now until I go to sleep tonight I will: _____

_____

_____

_____

Daily inventory

The last 24 hours I: _____

_____

_____

_____

_____

_____

_____

The Daily Self-report and Personal Inventory

Today I feel: _____

_____

_____

_____

Today I think: _____

_____

_____

_____

From now until I go to sleep tonight I will: _____

_____

_____

_____

Daily inventory

The last 24 hours I: _____

_____

_____

_____

_____

_____

The Daily Self-report and Personal Inventory

Today I feel: _____

_____

_____

_____

Today I think: _____

_____

_____

_____

From now until I go to sleep tonight I will: _____

_____

_____

_____

Daily inventory

The last 24 hours I: _____

_____

_____

_____

_____

_____

_____

The Daily Self-report and Personal Inventory

Today I feel: _____

_____

_____

_____

Today I think: _____

_____

_____

_____

From now until I go to sleep tonight I will: _____

_____

_____

_____

Daily inventory

The last 24 hours I: _____

_____

_____

_____

_____

_____

_____

The Daily Self-report and Personal Inventory

Today I feel: _____

_____

_____

_____

Today I think: _____

_____

_____

_____

From now until I go to sleep tonight I will: _____

_____

_____

_____

Daily inventory

The last 24 hours I: _____

_____

_____

_____

_____

_____

The Daily Self-report and Personal Inventory

Today I feel: _____

_____

_____

_____

Today I think: _____

_____

_____

_____

From now until I go to sleep tonight I will: _____

_____

_____

_____

Daily inventory

The last 24 hours I: _____

_____

_____

_____

_____

_____

The Daily Self-report and Personal Inventory

Today I feel: _____

_____

_____

_____

Today I think: _____

_____

_____

_____

From now until I go to sleep tonight I will: _____

_____

_____

_____

Daily inventory

The last 24 hours I: _____

_____

_____

_____

_____

_____

_____

The Daily Self-report and Personal Inventory

Today I feel: _____

_____

_____

_____

Today I think: _____

_____

_____

_____

From now until I go to sleep tonight I will: _____

_____

_____

_____

Daily inventory

The last 24 hours I: _____

_____

_____

_____

_____

_____

_____

The Daily Self-report and Personal Inventory

Today I feel: _____

_____

_____

_____

Today I think: _____

_____

_____

_____

From now until I go to sleep tonight I will: _____

_____

_____

_____

Daily inventory

The last 24 hours I: _____

_____

_____

_____

_____

_____

The Daily Self-report and Personal Inventory

Today I feel: _____

_____

_____

_____

Today I think: _____

_____

_____

_____

From now until I go to sleep tonight I will: _____

_____

_____

_____

Daily inventory

The last 24 hours I: _____

_____

_____

_____

_____

_____

_____

PART TWO

THE ART OF STRUGGLE REDUCTION

Reduce the Struggle

Think for a moment about how you would answer the next two questions. What would it feel like to spend most of the time, most days, living in peace? And what is preventing it?

The Art of Struggle Reduction provides a foundation for viewing life through a different lens. The concepts are easy to understand but can be challenging to implement. The reason is that the human mind is complicated, and The Art of Struggle Reduction is simple, very simple. One school of thought is that if you are not busy doing something and staying on top of things, you will lose your edge and your effectiveness. This attitude can create an over active mind, prone to excessive worry and stress. The Art of Struggle Reduction takes a different approach. Moving through life with minimal worry, stress, and struggle makes one more effective, not less. Imagine walking straight through an empty room to the other side instead of winding your way through piles of clutter. The heart of Struggle Reduction is less clutter. A mind that is settled and clear is at peace. Understanding replaces knowledge.

The methods we will discuss have been shown to be effective in helping to manage anger and stress, and helping to prevent relapse for those with substance use disorders and other mental health issues. Clients that do not learn how to manage and cope with anxiety and stress often relapsed, returning to the maladaptive pattern of self-medicating those uncomfortable feelings. There is a clear link among anxiety, stress, and relapse.

The Art of Struggle Reduction teaches the listener to observe his or her thoughts, identify areas of internal struggle, and utilize a few simple strategies—to allow the struggle to be reduced. The benefits are many: reduced anxiety, reduced frequency and intensity of panic attacks, less difficulty falling asleep at night, and a calmer lifestyle when awake. For the discussion of recovery from addiction, Struggle Reduction can be used to manage stress and anger which helps to prevent relapse. Regularly reaching a deep state of calm can help with overall health problems, such as lowering high blood pressure, and reducing the risk of stroke. These changes can potentially add years to your life. The bottom line is living a more calm, peaceful, relaxed life is good for your health.

SPECIFIC STRATEGIES AND METHODS OF STRUGGLE REDUCTION

The Water Globe

Visualize a water globe or snow globe. Imagine that each piece of glitter or snow floating in the water represents one of your thoughts. When you shake up the globe trying to make something happen, the glitter or snow moves about rapidly in a chaotic manor; however, if you sit the water globe down and just let it be, just observe it without intent, it becomes calm and still. Peace is a natural state, and when the mind is settled, peace exists. So, what causes the mind to become unsettled? Many forms of negative thinking and self-talk, irrational thoughts, worry, fear, obsessive guilt and shame, envy and jealously—simply put, it is our own internal struggle that kidnaps our minds from the awareness of peace. So, the question is not how does one find peace, but instead how does one reduce struggle. Come to understand why we struggle, and the struggle will cease.

Every moment of this day we have the choice to keep our hearts and souls open and aware of the peace that exists in the here and now, or to allow our minds to ignore this truth and get lost in the powerful negative energy that fuels anxiety and struggle. How you choose to spend your emotional energy from now until you go to sleep tonight will go far in determining the amount of peace in your life.

DTM Scale (Do the Math)

By observing your thoughts, you can identify areas of internal struggle. Then, utilizing a few simple methods and strategies, you can learn to reduce or release that struggle. Struggle exists both in the way we perceive external events and how those perceptions affect our internal dialog. Peace exists in the absence of struggle. Remember, the question is not how to find peace, but instead how to reduce struggle.

Every twenty-four hours, most of us spend five to eight hours sleeping. Of the remaining time, basically your time awake, how much is spent living in peace? And how much is spent living in struggle? Out of 100 percent of your time (16 to 19 hours per day), place a number that represents the average percent of time spent in struggle and another number representing the time spent at peace. Make sure both numbers add up to 100. You can use the following diagram for guidance. I've listed some examples; however, personalize it by adding your own in the spaces provided.

Struggle _____% worry, negative self-talk, fear, anger, quilt and shame, road rage, phobic, controlling, anxious, people-pleasing, overly critical, arguments with spouse or partner, problems with coworker

_____

_____

_____

_____

_____

Peace _____% relaxed, calm, happy, serene, enjoying life, worry-free, grateful, understanding, realistic self-talk, humility, loving, secure, accepting

_____

_____

_____

_____

Most people who do the math realize that 50 to 90 percent of their day is spent in some form of struggle. By increasing awareness and making some changes in thinking, these percentages can be adjusted. Try pausing several times a day to do the math. If you observe any struggle thinking, then it's time to make some decisions. The Art of Struggle Reduction offers 3 options. One, accept the situation exactly as it is then release the struggle. Two, take immediate action on a specific issue then release the struggle. And three, schedule a time later to resolve the situation and then release the struggle. Whether you decide to accept, act or delay, you can always choose to release the struggle and shift awareness to peace that exists in the present moment. With practice, a feeling of gaining more control over your life develops and you will begin taking joy in letting go of present moment struggle.

The Integrity Flower

The Integrity Flower exercise teaches us that when our outward behavior and actions don't match with the inner voice that guides us, there is struggle, and where there is struggle there is no peace. If you have a piece of paper and a pencil you could draw this out; otherwise, use your imagination. Imagine a flower with a large round center surrounded by small round petals. The large center circle of the flower represents the deepest part of us, our center and core of our being. Some would call it our soul, spirit, or heart. It is the inner voice that guides us. This is the place where we intuitively know right from wrong. The small round circles or petals represent our outward behavior and actions, the act of doing. Now take a self-inventory. How many of your actions are completely consistent with your innermost beliefs? By examining, and being brutally honest with yourself you can continue to make adjustments. As your outside actions become more in harmony with your inside beliefs, struggle falls away, and peace remains.

The goal here is to reduce struggle. In the world today, so many people live their lives in struggle with high levels of stress and anxiety. Some of the external challenges can seem very difficult. However, it is your perception of these events that will determine the amount of internal struggle you experience. With practice, it becomes easier to keep your awareness focused on the now and the peace that exists there.

Make a list of specific behaviors you would like to change to make them more consistent with your core beliefs.

_____

_____

_____

_____

Make Hills Out of The Mountain

Not being able to identify the various challenges in our lives can make it difficult to find solutions. By the time most people seek counseling for addiction and other mental health issues their ability to see the problems clearly has become clouded. It can begin to feel like everything has piled up and become one huge problem that is too big to handle. One huge mountain too large to climb. This robs us of motivation to work on solutions and keeps us stuck. We may even give up trying altogether. It can feel hopeless.

What is the answer? Start by making hills out of the mountain, they are much easier to travel. Each hill can be named and observed separately, for example: finances, relationship, employment etc. Deal with one hill or problem at a time rather than trying to tackle everything at once. Remember, whether you decide to accept, act, or delay, always choose to release the struggle and shift awareness to present moment peace.

Now answer these 2 questions:
If you are experiencing this problem, can you express how it makes you feel?

_____

_____

_____

_____

_____

_____

Can you identify and list areas in your life that are causing you struggle today?

_____

_____

_____

_____

Empty the Tank

Imagine that there are two separate tanks in your brain. One is used for processing events, and the other is used for storage. Everyday many different events occur in our lives. It is how we perceive and process these events and manage the feelings that will determine our level of struggle. For example; an event occurs. It is perceived and processed in the processing tank. Feelings are felt and managed, and then another event occurs, etc. If there is a problem with processing the event or managing the feelings, the unresolved content is moved to the storage tank where it could stay for hours, months, or even years. If the storage tank becomes full, the emotional content stored there begins to leak into the processing tank, disrupting the functioning there. It then becomes increasingly difficult to manage feelings, resulting in struggles with anxiety, fear, depression, anger and more. The solution is a dual process. Step one is to repair the processing tank by adjusting the way we perceive and process life's daily events. This will have a direct and positive impact on the feelings that are created, making them easier to manage. Increasing our struggle reduction methods will help keep the processing tank clean, clear, and functioning smoothly.

Step two is to observe specific content in the storage tank and then release the struggle. This will free up space. If we have done a good job with the first step, we won't be adding very much new content to the storage tank. And peace exists in the absence of struggle.

What irrational or impaired thinking do you use, on a daily basis that causes struggle?

_____

_____

_____

_____

What kind of thinking could you implement that would increase feelings of peace?

_____

_____

_____

_____

Can you identify anything in your storage tank that needs to be removed?

_____

_____

_____

_____

Identify and discuss specific strategies you can use to remove content from your storage tank.

_____

_____

_____

_____

Identify and list specific struggle reduction strategies to use in the here and now.

_____

_____

_____

_____

Some Thoughts on Relationship

Person A and person B are two separate and distinct individuals. Each has his or her own level of self-esteem, confidence, values, and ethics. They both have certain intuitive abilities to manage his or her emotions and behaviors with social supports for help. They each have their own interests, hobbies, hopes, and dreams. And both are on the path, as we all are, to receive the knowledge, insight, and understanding that life's journey will bring.

If person A and person B meet along the way, they may choose to walk the path together. They are two people on separate journeys walking the same path. They walk together because they have chosen to do so. They may come to care deeply for one another and form a rock-solid commitment to remain together on the path forever. Still they remain two people on separate journeys walking the same path.

In order for two separate and distinct individuals to walk the path together, they must learn the art of compromise. Debating ideas and beliefs is best done with empathy and compassion. Sadly, many strong feelings and emotions can cloud the view. It is important not to lose sight of the reason for compromise, and that is the choice to walk the path together. Compromise requires communication rooted in caring and respect for one another.

Many couples lose sight of caring compromise and become lost along the way. This is what lost looks like: saying or doing cruel things to each other, losing identity and becoming overly needy and dependent on each other. Lost looks like subjecting one another to physical or emotional pain, trying to control or force, and losing the ability to manage emotions and behaviors.

Love understands this. Love allows person A and person B to remain two separate and distinct individuals who have made the choice to travel the path together. Love shines a light so they can find the path if they get lost along the way. Love allows for each to want the other to experience his or her hopes and dreams to the fullest. Love provides strength and guidance to help them remain supportive of one another's journey, as they walk the path together.

Now answer these 3 questions:
Can you identify any struggles in your relationships?

_____

_____

_____

_____

What specific changes could you make to improve the relationship?

_____

_____

_____

_____

_____

What specific changes would you like to see your partner make?

_____

_____

_____

_____

_____

Meditation

I would like to present a very simple view on the topic of meditation. Less is more. When listening to music it is not necessarily the notes that create the rhythm or feel of the song, it is the space between the notes. Assume a comfortable sitting position, close your eyes, take a few deep breaths, smile, and relax. Soon you may begin to notice the thoughts racing around in your mind. Trying to slow your thoughts down or clear your mind of them all together just creates struggle. Where there is struggle, there is no peace. Instead, just relax and observe without intent. Visualize that you are watching a movie and your thoughts are the movie's scenes flashing across the big screen. If you can relax and observe without struggle, allowing the thoughts to come and go peacefully, the thoughts will begin to slow down on their own with no effort on your part. In fact, effort on your part will just stir them up. As the thoughts begin to slow, your awareness of peace begins to increase. This can take up to 15 or 20 minutes, but the centering down time decreases with practice.

It may take several attempts to develop a comfort level with this process as most people are not used to sitting still without activity. But that is what this meditation consists of. As you continue to sit with eyes closed and a relaxed attitude, the increased awareness of peace just happens. When one comes to understand this on a deeper level, anxiety and worry is reduced. After all what is there to worry about, all you are doing is sitting and observing. Everything occurs naturally, without effort. Why not try going to the "movies" tonight.

Deep Relaxation

One of the most effective ways to manage anxiety and stress is to learn how to relax. Not just relaxing as in "kicking back" and reading a good book, but learning how to reach a deep state of relaxation. Some of the methods for achieving this are guided visualization, meditation, and progressive muscle relaxation.

Progressive muscle relaxation, or PMR, was discovered and introduced by Dr. Edmund Jacobson. This technique involves tensing and relaxing various major muscle groups throughout the body in what some refer to as "bringing the body down." Guided visualization and meditation can help ease the mind into harmony with the relaxed body. A good way to look at it is, "bring the body down and the mind will follow."

The term "guided relaxation" refers to a recorded voice-over that explains to and guides the listener. As with any guided relaxation, the listener is encouraged to assume a comfortable position and close their eyes. It is important to remember not to try to force a state of calm or clearing of the mind, as that only creates struggle. Instead, just relax, smile, and allow the relaxation to unfold. The body and mind will naturally settle and become still. Remember to take slow, deep breaths during the practice. When the session is over, the participant usually experiences a relaxed feeling, both physically and emotionally. The mind and body become accustomed to deep relaxation, and with regular practice, moving easily into a deep state of calm.

You can listen to and practice guided relaxation on the www.meditationalbums.com website. I recommend practicing relaxation daily, for four to six weeks. The practice may then be adjusted as needed. If your anxiety level increases, try increasing the number of sessions. Also, on nights when you have difficulty falling asleep, practicing deep relaxation will often put you right to sleep. In my experience, this practice of guided relaxation has been especially helpful to those with addiction problems and certain types of anxiety disorders.

Progressive Muscle Relaxation Script

Progressive muscle relaxation can be effectively utilized as needed to help reduce stress, as maintenance in a relaxation program, and to help induce sleep. The technique is simple and involves the tightening and relaxing of muscle groups throughout the body. First, we will tighten a specific muscle group, and then bring your awareness to how the muscle feels when tense. Hold it for seven seconds, release it suddenly, and bring your awareness to how the muscle now feels relaxed. Follow this with a deep breath to the bottom of your lungs. Tensing and relaxing various muscle groups throughout the body can help produce a deep state of calm. Let's begin by closing our eyes and taking a deep breath. As you breathe in and out, allow your worries and concerns to drift away. Now, let's begin with the muscles around your eyes and forehead. Tighten the muscles and hold it 1, 2, 3, 4, 5, 6, 7, and release, deep breath. Press your tongue against the roof of your mouth and tighten your jaw muscles, 1, 2, 3, 4, 5, 6, 7, and release. Allow your muscles to relax and your mouth to hang open. Now push your shoulders up, trying to touch your ears, and hold it, 1, 2, 3, 4, 5, 6, 7, and release, deep breath. Move to the muscles in your upper back, try to push your shoulder blades together and hold it 1, 2, 3, 4, 5, 6, 7, and release, deep breath. Moving to your right arm we tighten the bicep, triceps, wrist and hand, tightening them all and hold it 1, 2, 3, 4, 5, 6, 7, release. Now, we'll do the same thing with our left arm the bicep, triceps, wrist and hand tensing all the muscles and hold it 1, 2, 3, 4, 5, 6, 7, release, deep breath. As you move to the muscles in your stomach, you begin to feel your upper body becoming heavy and calm. Tighten your stomach muscles and hold it, 1, 2, 3, 4, 5, 6, 7, and release. As the tensions continue to leave your muscles, you feel your body relaxing more and more. Next, we move to our right leg. Tighten your thigh, calf all the way down to your ankle and hold it, 1, 2, 3, 4, 5, 6, 7, release, deep breath. Moving to our left leg we tighten the thigh, calf, and down to the ankle tensing them all and hold it, 1, 2, 3, 4, 5, 6, 7, and release, deep breath. Your body is heavy. Your mind is calm as you drift deeper and deeper into total relaxation.

From Now Until You Go to Sleep

Prior to a musical performance, the band will often do a dress rehearsal or sound check. They perform a part of the regular show, making sure everything is in tune and functioning. The musicians and crew adjust volumes, aim lighting, and basically prepare for the show that will take place later. Many people spend their time on earth in a dress rehearsal, preparing to live their life. It sounds like this: "One of these days, I'm going to..." or, "Someday I will get around to that..." Blame is often assigned to someone or something: "If I could just get out of this relationship..." or, "When I finally get a better job..." The Art of Struggle Reduction teaches us to live in the present moment and take responsibility for our choices. A phrase often used in Struggle Reduction is "from now until I go to sleep tonight."

Each moment, you can decide to release the struggle and be aware of peace. It's your decision what type of morals you will live by and if your actions will be in harmony with the inner voice that guides you. You will choose how much time you spend worrying about what other people think of you. From now until you go to sleep tonight, live the life you want, in peace, and with meaning and purpose. It is your choice, and this is not a dress rehearsal.

From now until I go to sleep tonight, this is how I choose to live my life

_____

_____

_____

_____

_____

_____

_____

_____

_____

_____

Re-establish Your Baseline

For the purpose of this book, the term baseline refers to the place where one feels the most emotionally stable and well. Think of one of those days when you are moving through life with the wind at your back and a clear view of the peace that exists in the here and now. The numbers 1, 2, and 3 represent three different individuals with varying levels of anxiety. Person 1 in our example experiences a mild amount of anxiety based on his or her perceptions of life's events. This anxiety moves them a short distance from their baseline. However, person number one has the coping skills to manage and return to his or her baseline. Person 2, on the other hand, finds life's events much more difficult to manage. Moderate anxiety has moved him or her much further from their baseline causing considerable discomfort. It is with much struggle that this person is able to find and return to his or her baseline. Finally, person number three has minimal ability to cope at this time and struggles to even remember what the baseline feels like. High anxiety has moved this person to a very scary place, and he or she cannot find the way back.

Baseline

1 Mild anxiety, uneasy feelings

2 Moderate anxiety, very uncomfortable

3 High anxiety, panic, extreme fear

When anxiety reaches high levels, the goal is to reduce it enough to re-establish some comfort with the baseline. Re-discovering your baseline after having been out on an emotional limb is like a drop of water in the desert. The increased awareness of peace, along with the relaxation and meditation techniques featured in this book, will help many re-establish their baseline. You may need to seek the help of a licensed mental health counselor or psychiatrist if the anxiety persists at a high level. As you learn how to incorporate the principles of Struggle Reduction into your life, the Baseline chart and the DTM scale in chapter 3 can be used as helpful guides.

Oneness

I remember as a child laying in the yard, on my back, feeling and smelling the earth and grass. Gazing up at the sky, I would watch the beautiful white clouds slowly morph from one shape to the next. First, I could see a dinosaur, then a tree, and then a car. With no beginning or ending, the slow continual movement of the clouds created a playground right in front of my eyes. I remember a feeling of oneness with the earth and sky, as time seemed to stand still. Totally present in the moment, there was no regretting the past, or worry for the future. There was not even a conscious awareness of self. Everything was connected. The warm summer breeze was the artist, creating an ever-changing display of fascinating objects. There was peace and happiness. Not a care in the world.

I still experience those moments as an adult, maybe on a lovely summer day, playing in the yard with my children or walking on the sandy beach, listening to the hypnotic sound of the ocean waves. Often during silent meditation or deep relaxation, life just opens up, and that feeling of oneness occurs, accompanied by total joy and peace. There is a very natural feel to it. It just is. And I wonder if everything else is some type of struggle, in one form or another.

Practicing the Art of Struggle Reduction

Sometime during each day, sit down and close your eyes. Next, take a few deep breaths and observe your thoughts. Don't try to clear your mind or change anything, just observe without intent. Don't push or exert, just relax and observe for several minutes. Then using the DTM journal on the following pages, list any peaceful or struggle thinking that you observed. In the space provided, write a few notes about your thoughts. Remember, there is no right or wrong way to do this. This is not a test or competition. Just a flowing, effortless, awareness of how you are using your emotional energy. Doesn't it make sense to shift your awareness away from any struggle thinking?

Then, in the evening, journal about your perceptions of the day's events. How did those perceptions affect your feelings? Doesn't it make sense to shift your awareness from negative struggle thinking to positive peaceful thoughts?

We have included 30 daily DTM Scores. This will be sufficient for the first month. Feel free to make copies for ongoing use.

DTM SCORE

Struggle _____ %

Notes: _____

_____

_____

_____

_____

Peace _____%

Notes: _____

_____

_____

_____

_____

SELF-REPORT

In the past 24 hours, I: _____

_____

_____

_____

_____

_____

_____

_____

DTM SCORE

Struggle _____ %

Notes: _____

_____

_____

_____

_____

Peace _____%

Notes: _____

_____

_____

_____

_____

SELF-REPORT

In the past 24 hours, I: _____

_____

_____

_____

_____

_____

_____

_____

DTM SCORE

Struggle _____ %

Notes: _____

_____

_____

_____

_____

Peace _____%

Notes: _____

_____

_____

_____

_____

SELF-REPORT

In the past 24 hours, I: _____

_____

_____

_____

_____

_____

_____

_____

DTM SCORE

Struggle _____ %

Notes: _____

_____

_____

_____

_____

Peace _____%

Notes: _____

_____

_____

_____

_____

SELF-REPORT

In the past 24 hours, I: _____

_____

_____

_____

_____

_____

_____

_____

DTM SCORE

Struggle _____ %

Notes: _____

_____

_____

_____

Peace _____%

Notes: _____

_____

_____

_____

SELF-REPORT

In the past 24 hours, I: _____

_____

_____

_____

_____

_____

_____

DTM SCORE

Struggle _____ %

Notes: _____

_____

_____

_____

_____

Peace _____ %

Notes: _____

_____

_____

_____

_____

SELF-REPORT

In the past 24 hours, I: _____

_____

_____

_____

_____

_____

_____

_____

DTM SCORE

Struggle _____ %

Notes: _____

_____

_____

_____

_____

Peace _____%

Notes: _____

_____

_____

_____

SELF-REPORT

In the past 24 hours, I: _____

_____

_____

_____

_____

_____

_____

_____

DTM SCORE

Struggle _____ %

Notes: _____

_____

_____

_____

_____

Peace _____%

Notes: _____

_____

_____

_____

_____

SELF-REPORT

In the past 24 hours, I: _____

_____

_____

_____

_____

_____

_____

_____

DTM SCORE

Struggle _____ %

Notes: _____

_____

_____

_____

_____

Peace _____%

Notes: _____

_____

_____

_____

_____

SELF-REPORT

In the past 24 hours, I: _____

_____

_____

_____

_____

_____

_____

DTM SCORE

Struggle _____ %

Notes: _____

_____

_____

_____

_____

Peace _____%

Notes: _____

_____

_____

_____

_____

SELF-REPORT

In the past 24 hours, I: _____

_____

_____

_____

_____

_____

_____

_____

DTM SCORE

Struggle _____ %

Notes: _____

_____

_____

_____

_____

Peace _____%

Notes: _____

_____

_____

_____

_____

SELF-REPORT

In the past 24 hours, I: _____

_____

_____

_____

_____

_____

_____

DTM SCORE

Struggle _____ %

Notes: _____

_____

_____

_____

_____

Peace _____%

Notes: _____

_____

_____

_____

_____

SELF-REPORT

In the past 24 hours, I: _____

_____

_____

_____

_____

_____

_____

_____

DTM SCORE

Struggle _____ %

Notes: _____

_____

_____

_____

_____

Peace _____%

Notes: _____

_____

_____

_____

_____

SELF-REPORT

In the past 24 hours, I: _____

_____

_____

_____

_____

_____

_____

_____

DTM SCORE

Struggle _____ %

Notes: _____

_____

_____

_____

_____

Peace _____%

Notes: _____

_____

_____

_____

_____

SELF-REPORT

In the past 24 hours, I: _____

_____

_____

_____

_____

_____

_____

_____

DTM SCORE

Struggle _____ %

Notes: _____

_____

_____

_____

_____

Peace _____%

Notes: _____

_____

_____

_____

_____

SELF-REPORT

In the past 24 hours, I: _____

_____

_____

_____

_____

_____

_____

DTM SCORE

Struggle _____ %

Notes: _____

_____

_____

_____

_____

Peace _____%

Notes: _____

_____

_____

_____

_____

SELF-REPORT

In the past 24 hours, I: _____

_____

_____

_____

_____

_____

_____

_____

DTM SCORE

Struggle _____ %

Notes: _____

_____

_____

_____

_____

Peace _____%

Notes: _____

_____

_____

_____

SELF-REPORT

In the past 24 hours, I: _____

_____

_____

_____

_____

_____

_____

DTM SCORE

Struggle _____ %

Notes: _____

_____

_____

_____

_____

Peace _____%

Notes: _____

_____

_____

_____

_____

SELF-REPORT

In the past 24 hours, I: _____

_____

_____

_____

_____

_____

_____

_____

DTM SCORE

Struggle _____ %

Notes: _____

_____

_____

_____

_____

Peace _____%

Notes: _____

_____

_____

_____

_____

SELF-REPORT

In the past 24 hours, I: _____

_____

_____

_____

_____

_____

_____

_____

DTM SCORE

Struggle _____ %

Notes: _____

_____

_____

_____

_____

Peace _____%

Notes: _____

_____

_____

_____

_____

SELF-REPORT

In the past 24 hours, I: _____

_____

_____

_____

_____

_____

_____

_____

DTM SCORE

Struggle _____ %

Notes: _____

_____

_____

_____

_____

Peace _____%

Notes: _____

_____

_____

_____

_____

SELF-REPORT

In the past 24 hours, I: _____

_____

_____

_____

_____

_____

_____

_____

DTM SCORE

Struggle _____ %

Notes: _____

_____

_____

_____

_____

Peace _____%

Notes: _____

_____

_____

_____

_____

SELF-REPORT

In the past 24 hours, I: _____

_____

_____

_____

_____

_____

_____

_____

DTM SCORE

Struggle _____ %

Notes: _____

_____

_____

_____

_____

Peace _____%

Notes: _____

_____

_____

_____

_____

SELF-REPORT

In the past 24 hours, I: _____

_____

_____

_____

_____

_____

_____

_____

DTM SCORE

Struggle _____ %

Notes: _____

_____

_____

_____

_____

Peace _____%

Notes: _____

_____

_____

_____

_____

SELF-REPORT

In the past 24 hours, I: _____

_____

_____

_____

_____

_____

_____

_____

DTM SCORE

Struggle _____ %

Notes: _____

_____

_____

_____

_____

Peace _____%

Notes: _____

_____

_____

_____

_____

SELF-REPORT

In the past 24 hours, I: _____

_____

_____

_____

_____

_____

_____

_____

DTM SCORE

Struggle _____ %

Notes: _____

_____

_____

_____

_____

Peace _____%

Notes: _____

_____

_____

_____

_____

SELF-REPORT

In the past 24 hours, I: _____

_____

_____

_____

_____

_____

_____

_____

DTM SCORE

Struggle _____ %

Notes: _____

_____

_____

_____

_____

Peace _____%

Notes: _____

_____

_____

_____

_____

SELF-REPORT

In the past 24 hours, I: _____

_____

_____

_____

_____

_____

_____

_____

DTM SCORE

Struggle _____ %

Notes: _____

_____

_____

_____

_____

Peace _____%

Notes: _____

_____

_____

_____

_____

SELF-REPORT

In the past 24 hours, I: _____

_____

_____

_____

_____

_____

_____

_____

DTM SCORE

Struggle _____ %

Notes: _____

_____

_____

_____

_____

Peace _____%

Notes: _____

_____

_____

_____

_____

SELF-REPORT

In the past 24 hours, I: _____

_____

_____

_____

_____

_____

_____

_____

DTM SCORE

Struggle _____ %

Notes: _____

_____

_____

_____

_____

Peace _____%

Notes: _____

_____

_____

_____

_____

SELF-REPORT

In the past 24 hours, I: _____

_____

_____

_____

_____

_____

_____

_____

72468305R00070

Made in the USA
Lexington, KY
30 November 2017